THE POCKET GUIDE TO

FISHING KNOTS

A STEP-BY-STEP GUIDE TO THE MOST IMPORTANT KNOTS FOR FRESH AND SALT WATER

JOSEPH B. HEALY

Skyhorse Publishing

Skyhorse Publishing books may be purchased in bulk at special discounts
for sales promotion, corporate gifts, fund-raising, or educational purposes.
Special editions can also be created to specifications. For details, contact
the Special Sales Department, Skyhorse Publishing, 307 West 36th Street,
11th Floor, New York, NY 10018 or info@skyhorsepublishing.com.

Skyhorse® and Skyhorse Publishing® are registered trademarks of
Skyhorse Publishing, Inc.®, a Delaware corporation.

Visit our website at www.skyhorsepublishing.com.

10 9 8 7 6 5 4 3

Library of Congress Cataloging-in-Publication Data is available on file.

Cover design by Tom Lau

Print ISBN: 978-1-5107-2121-0
Ebook ISBN: 978-1-5107-2122-7

Printed in China

Contents

Preface: Why Knots?

In the Skyhorse series of *Pocket Guide to ... Knots* books, we pose the question right from the get-go: Why knots? Today, we have all manner of fastener systems and glues by which anyone can affix one thing to another. Velcro, snaps, fasteners, buckles, super glue, epoxy—all can do the job for us, right?

Not so much in fishing applications. We want to work with our hands and our minds when fishing—we want the tactile feel of being connected to a wild thing and the satisfaction of knowing that we created the connections by which we're joined. Also, fishing is a craft of skill, and isn't it more fulfilling to develop the muscle memory that enables us to loop, twist, and thread lines together to form an unbreakable knot? Sure it is. We're really endeavoring to create unbreakable bonds, which is a philosophical or spiritual, or even metaphorical, truth. Part of fishing—or equestrian or prepping skills, to mention two other subjects in the Skyhorse Pocket Knot series—is being ready and able to join lines for specific purposes, anytime you want, either while preparing to fish away from the water at the boat dock or in your garage, or while you're waist-deep wading in a river, or sitting in a kayak or a canoe, or lounging on a shoreline. Here's another thought: We don't need any gizmos when we've got two hands and a brain and can learn the skills that call to mind the slogan "be prepared." Being an angler means being prepared for any line fixes, at any time. Further, fishing is a challenge of experimentation and exploration and discovery. Knots bind us to that, too.

I think back on a trip to the Black Hills of South Dakota, when I was driving with determination to get to Sioux Falls for an early flight the next morning after fishing in Yellowstone National Park and spending time in Montana and Wyoming. In the afternoon, I had to take a break from driving—and I needed to fish. I stopped at a well-worn parking area and slipped on my waders and fishing vest and assembled my 6-weight fly rod. No one was around, it was about two in the afternoon on an August day. I walked down to the stream, a meander leading into a pond. A beaten path encircled the pond, which probably attracted most of the fishing attention at that pullout. I followed the stream up, against its current, away from the pond. After fifty yards or so, I saw a long shadow—but it moved, undulating side to side. It was a massive trout. Perhaps this stream was stocked? I saw "catch-and-release only/artificial flies only" signs along the path. Special regulations, a signal this was special trout water. I watched the fish as it held in a deep pool, and it eased to the surface, gently eating something and leaving a dimple in the flat water. I looked closer into the water and saw cream-colored mayflies on the surface. A big fish meant serious food, so rather than try to match the hatch, I tied on a meaty grasshopper pattern. I was amped—like buck fever for hunters, I had big-trout fever. With shaking hands, I hurried to tie on the hopper imitation. I cast upstream of the fish and mended the fly line slightly as the hopper drifted down toward the fish. I saw a slight shift in the fish's attitude—maybe it took a look at the fake hopper, but it wasn't convinced? I cast again, flipping a mend in the line to the right and then left, and steered the fly to the outskirts of the fish's vision. It did not hesitate—it streaked sideways and swirled at the surface to engulf my Joe's Hopper. I brought up my rod, tightening the line and bending the rod. I had a solid hookset . . . for about twenty seconds. The fish swirled away toward a deadfall near the streambank and I flexed the rod to try and turn the fish's momentum. And my knot pulled free: My fly and the fish were gone. It was big fish, probably a cut-throat trout or a cut-bow hybrid. Of course, I'll never know what it was. I had a curlicue on the end of my tippet, the tell-tale sign that the knot pulled free. It was supposed to be an Improved Clinch Knot, but I had messed up something in my haste to tie it. After that, I methodically rededicated myself to tying dependable knots. Since that time, I haven't had another Improved Clinch fail me, and that was about sixteen years ago. I've caught striped bass, bluefish, tarpon, per-mit, snook, grouper, bonefish, sea trout, redfish, brown, brook, and rainbow trout, bass, pike, and panfish—all without knot failures, at least not at the terminal knot where the tippet is tied to the fly. Why knots? That's why. I learned the knots I needed, I practiced and improved, I committed the tying instructions to my muscle memory (to the point where I can tie most fishing knots at night in the dark), and I have many fine memo-ries of great days catching wonderful fish. No snaps, fasteners, or glues necessary. "A fisherman is only as good as his (or her) knots" is a common truism. More accurately, fisherman will never land a fish if they don't master basic knots. You may hook or "sting" a fish, as in my anecdote above, but you won't achieve that satisfaction of landing and releasing or keeping the fish, whatever your preference. Knots are foundations of fishing, you need to learn them, just as you need to learn where to find fish in a stream or how to read the tides to know where fish might be in the ocean. We need knots—they complete our connections.

Introduction

I fell in love with the idea and concept of fly fishing many years before I actually began to fly fish. I grew up on a lake in Central New York, jigging for walleyes, casting Hula-Poppers for bass, and ice-fishing. Before that, I dunked worms for trout in area rivers. But even as a child, I always wanted to fly fish.

For the curious conventional-tackle angler like younger me, fly fishing seemed more of a natural way to connect with the environment, it seemed more skilled than my jigging. Little did I know how good it would get, or where the craft would eventually take me. I've caught tarpon in the Florida Keys, silver salmon in Alaska, permit in Mexico, bonefish in Belize, Atlantic salmon in Ireland. All on flies.

I don't particularly like writing the above words, especially because fly fishing has also given me humility. I thrive on the connections with other anglers, with being part of the environment, with the fish (of course), with the movement and physical mechanics of casting, and with the intellectual challenge of discerning what the fish are eating . . . I truly love all that. I also feel gratified by the technical, endemic knowledge I've acquired along the way, a big portion of which includes knot tying. As my friend Phil Monahan points out in this book, the most difficult knots can—strangely—be the most gratifying to tie. I don't include any truly impossible knots in this book. Phil is speaking of the Albright Knot (also known as the Albright Special)—a knot Phil ties well. And when Phil gives me a chance to tie it—

he volunteered to be my designated Albright tier for a number of years when we worked together—I feel gratified by the having the skill to do it, too.

I feel grateful to share the voices you'll hear in this book—from anglers such as Flip Pallot, Jimmy Houston, Tom Rosenbauer, Steve Pennaz, Chico Fernandez, Jerry Gibbs, and others. Those interviewed for their knot insights in this book are not only great anglers, they're also great human beings, and I am blessed to know them. Read and reflect on the advice they give. And, most important, practice your knot tying, using the illustrations in this book. It's fun and gratifying (though maybe frustrating at the start), and each time you land a fish, whether it's a ten-pound walleye or a hundred-pound tarpon, you'll be pleased with the knot-tying knowledge you possess.

When it comes to refining that knot knowledge and solidifying your muscle memory of tying knots, I'm reminded of a fishing experience I had while I was a journalist riding aboard Capt. Randy Towe's flats boat in Islamorada, Florida, as Randy was guiding angler Pat Ford in the Golden Fly Tarpon Tournament one spring. Pat had caught a tarpon of about 155 pounds first thing in the morning, and hooked a second fish of probably about 120 pounds when his connection failed and the shock tippet came back with a curlicue. It happens, even to an angler of Pat's vast experience; he has held umpteen International Game Fish Association records, including one for cobia that will likely stand for a long time—a sixty-seven-pound, four-ounce cobia on fly tackle, in the eight-pound test line class. He says the only things that connect you to a fish are the knots in your fishing lines—and those connections are only as good as you make them. He puts is plainly: "If you've got a bad knot anywhere in your connection, the line is only as strong as that knot. There's nothing more important than your knots."

Pat offers the recommendation that anglers learn three knots—or three types of knots: a loop knot, an Improved Clinch Knot when you don't use a loop, and something that connects leader sections. "You need to figure out a sequence for using those knots," he says, "and you need to know those knots really well. That's all based on the premise that the only thing connecting you to the fish are the knots."

Here's more input on knots—and a preview of the interviews in this book—from an angling friend and a tremendous fly fisher.

Knot Know-How

with Sandy Moret, Islamorada, Florida

Sandy and wife Sue own and operate Florida Keys Outfitters in Islamorada, for decades one of the most influential fly-fishing shops in the Florida Keys. Sandy has won the Keys' most prestigious fly-fishing tournaments nine times, and he's a catalyst in teaching the sport through the Florida Keys Fly Fishing School, organized by his shop.

"There have been a plethora of knots through the years, and that has led to a tremendous amount

of confusion, and the development of specialty knots for this and that. But when I first started fishing in salt water in the Florida Keys and South Florida back in 1972, I got involved with Miami and sport-fishing clubs, and kept up with the Salt Water Fly Rodders of America, who maintained records until the IGFA (International Game Fish Association) took over. I got involved in fishing some of the tournaments in the Keys. I found I got lucky more often than not, and that was encouraging.

"But the confusion and lack of understanding of the importance of knots was something we had to wade through back then, and I found a couple things: You needed to attach a butt section to a fly line, and that led to tying a Nail Knot, which is basically the same as a Uni-Knot or Duncan Loop. The Nail Knot was as important back then as now, although you didn't have to tie it often. If you tied a good, eight-turn Nail Knot and used no more than the twenty-pound (ten kilogram) maximum tippet according to the rules of fly fishing, you weren't going to have any problems with it coming loose. It was pretty fail-safe. About twenty years ago, we learned to tie the same knot without the nail and the Nail-less Nail Knot was developed, thus destroying a micro industry because nobody needed all those Nail Knot tools anymore. Of course, we always used a paperclip for our Nail Knots.

"The other thing a Nail Knot allows you to do is to put a loop in the end of your fly line. You can use two Nail Knots with fifteen-pound mono and a little space between them to make a loop for connecting your fly line to your backing. That's a no-fail system. The Nail Knot is versatile in that way." (See that knot on page 147 in this book.)

Sandy continues: "The next thing you have to do is join two pieces of monofilament of similar sizes to taper a leader. I found a Blood Knot is the best knot for this. I guess it's called a Blood Knot because when you tighten it you can cut your hand. It's really two Clinch Knots tied back to back, if you think about it. It's simple. An improved Blood Knot can be used with dissimilar diameter lines. Same knot, just double the light line and treat it as one piece. You have to remember to always wrap the lighter line more times than the heavier line. This is because the lighter line compresses easier and faster. When that knot ties up tight, there should be no space and no give. And the tag ends can be cut totally flush, so no tags are hanging out. That doesn't sound like a big issue, but the fact that you can cut those tags and not pick up a piece of grass when you're fishing is a huge issue. A Blood Knot is a must knot. We teach those in the Florida Keys Outfitters school."

Sandy humbly mentions that he learned much of this in the Islamorada Bonefish Tournament, "fishing for the biggest, smartest bonefish on the planet, where a ten-pound bonefish barely gets a look." Sandy speaks the truth: that's the toughest bonefish tournament anywhere, and Sandy's won it five times.

Of course, in this equation, you still have to tie the hook on your tippet. Sandy recommends using an Improved Clinch or a Duncan Loop to do so. "Those are the knots I use. I have a lot of confidence in them; they're proven and they're simple. I'm a firm believer that one of the joys of fly fishing is the fact that it's so simple. When you become a competent caster, it's almost like you reach out and place the fly and coax and trigger the fish into a strike response. There's no scent, there's no trickery—it's just a pure and simple interaction with nature and a creature."

For tarpon and big game, Sandy uses a Bimini Twist to form the double line and class tippet. The double line is tied to the leader butt section or a taper with an Improved Blood Knot, as is the single stand of tippet to the shock or bite tippet. "It's a pretty simple operation," Sandy says. "When you tie the same knots and they work, you get more confidence in them, you tie them better, and you pull harder against them." Amen to that.

Proficiency in tying knots is critical to fishing success, but so is maintaining your connections and inspecting your leaders throughout a fishing day. No less an authority than Joe Brooks of *Outdoor Life* wrote in his book *Salt Water Fly Fishing*, first published in 1950: "The leader requires a minimum of care but that minimum is extremely important." He recommended feeling along the leader after landing a fish, to check for nicks and cuts; if needed, cut away the weakened part of the leader and retie. Periodically retie your hook, as casting can weaken the terminal connection, Brooks advised. "All these things take only a minute to do and may save you many a nice fish," he wrote. Remember—this was first published in 1950!

A friend of Brooks, Ben O. Williams of Livingston, Montana, reminisced with me about visiting with him in the 1960s and '70s. Ben worked at Dan Bailey's Fly Shop in Livingston during his summers off from teaching school, and he met many outdoor legends, such as Brooks, Lee Wulff, and Charlie Waterman. (And Ben's no angling slouch himself.) He recalls, "I started tying knots when I was a kid in the Boy Scouts. I've always been fascinated with knots. Then, I joined the Navy and I learned every knot you could possibly tie because it was required." He says even when he was teaching drafting or science classes at school, he would address the importance of knots. He credits Brooks with teaching so many. Ben suggests using a section of clothesline or other thick rope when practicing knots so you can visually see them coming together: "You want to see what the knot really does."

Another inveterate angler and friend who I met through editorial work is Jerry Hamza, author of *Outdoor Chronicles* (available from Skyhorse Publishing), and a brother from another mother who grew up in Central-Western New York, the same region I did. He says he uses two knots in fly fishing—a Nail Knot to assemble a leader, and the Improved Clinch Knot for the terminal connection. He jokingly (I think) adds that it helps to tighten down the Super Improved Clinch Knot (his name for the Improved Clinch) if you've had a Scotch and that mixes with your saliva, but he says it has to be good Scotch, otherwise it's a Barely Improved Clinch Knot. He feels the Improved Clinch Knot is dependable and has been around so long simply because it works. Jerry's fished around the world for countless species (which you can read about in *Outdoor Chronicles*).

All the knots included in this book are tried-and-true. You may find a couple that best fit your fishing. Practice and master them, since you'll want to be able to tie them in the dark, when it's cold, in rough seas in a boat, or on the shore when it's windy, or on a cloudy day in flat light. Study them, tie them, fish them—find success.

Joe Healy
Waterford, Vermont
Spring 2017

Looking at Fishing Lines

From the time when anglers began to appreciate catching fish as a sport, and not only as a skill used to harvest food, the earliest fishing lines were reported to be made of horsehair and gut, later giving way to silk—the era was the seventeenth and eighteenth centuries. These silk lines were cast with a whippy pole or rod, the precursor to a fly rod. Later, silk bait-casting lines became popular. The leader on the horsehair or silk line was gut, a material which was less obvious to fish when underwater and therefore less of a threat to fish than the heavier silk casting line to which it was attached. The leader was the transitional piece of the connection intended to be as translucent as possible so the fish might be fooled into eating the fly or bait. This principle of using a line less visible or at least less noticeable to fish paved the way for the nearly invisible lines such as today's monofilament (a single strand of extruded nylon, hence the name monofilament) or fluorocarbon used as the terminal fishing connection. As noted fishing writer A. J. McClane told readers in his classic book *The Practical Fly Fisherman*, "The purpose of a leader is to reduce the visible connection between line and fly. Obviously, the trout, a fish credited with keen eyesight, is going to be suspicious of his breakfast if something is leading it around by the nose." So, we heighten our deception by adding a section of line that disappears or blends in with the surroundings, or does both.

Still, an angler must first decide on a type of fishing line based on the application. It used to

be a fishing line was dried after use, to pro-
tect it from wearing thin or rotting. In *Tackle
Tinkering*, H. G. Tapply writes about allowing a
fishing line to dry on a piece of newspaper—in
fact, he recommends that method. (Although
H. G. cautions "remember, when drying, to keep
the line out of the sun and away from direct
heat.") That book was published in the 1940s.
I've been lucky in my career as an outdoors
editor, and one shining friendship was getting
to know Bill Tapply, the son of H. G. Tapply (also
known as Tap). I never told Bill this truth . . . that
I learned to read from studying "Tap's Tips" in
Field & Stream. Quite literally, I was probably
three or four years old at the time—though it
wouldn't have been the first time Bill had heard
that, no doubt. Generations loved Tap and his
outdoor tips. (Other readers loved Bill, for he
was a talented mystery novelist, as well as a
gifted outdoor storyteller.) H. G. takes us deep-
er into history when writing about dressing
bait-casting lines with beeswax, paraffin, or fly-
line dressing. The same was true for fly lines of

the 1940s—they needed to be dressed before use. I won't go into H. G.'s advice for detecting breaks in a fly-line surface and repairing the line. Refinishing a HDG or GAF fly line in that era was tedious and time-consuming and never guaranteed saving the line. Even knowing the kind and size of line you were using required some guesswork or mathematics with the use of a micrometer. Back then, anglers tried to follow guidelines from the National Association of Angling and Casting Clubs to determine a uniform system of fly-line size—I say "tried to follow" because lots of variance existed depending on the type of line.

Speaking of the alphabetic soup of fly-line designations back in the mid-twentieth century, we learn from *The Practical Fly Fisherman* by A. J. McClane about the actual letter-size designations of fly lines back then, which accounted for the names of the lines such as HDH or HCH or GBG and FAF. For hoots and giggles, as they say, let's take a look:

LETTER SIZE	NOMINAL DIAMETERS (In 1000th of Inch)
I	.022
H	.025
G	.030
F	.035
E	.040
D	.045
C	.050
B	.055
A	.066
AA	.065
AAA	.070
AAAA	.075
AAAAA	.080

As such, a double-taper fly line recommended for an 8 ½-foot, 5-ounce fly rod might be HDH, whereas a so-called three-diameter line would be HCF, McClane tells us. My point here is to consider the naming convention of that time, and to appreciate how we've simplified matters through the decades—at least when it comes to fly lines.

Nowadays, we buy fly lines by their number rating—5- and 6-weights for trout, for example, and 8- to 12-weights and up for heavier fish in fresh and salt water. The heavier lines help us cast in windy conditions or when we need to make long-distance casts to wary fish on the alert for predators (including anglers, you might say). The numbers are based on the grain weight of the head of the line, the forward-most thirty feet.

The constant between then and now when assembling your tackle connections is the need for dependable knots, such as two that McClane shares in his book that you'll also find in this book—the Blood Knot (for joining leader sections) and the Perfection Loop (for making loops in the ends of leader sections if you want to use loop-to-loop connections). H. G. Tapply also lists knots in *Tackle Tinkering* (1946), in a chapter titled "Knots: Hitches and Splices the Angler Should Know": He shares the Perfection Loop and also the Barrel Knot (similar to the Blood Knot) and

Cortland's best-selling freshwater fly line, the Classic 444 weight-forward line. Use loop-to-loop connections to attach the fly line to the braided backing and the leader butt.

Cortland's Big Fly line has welded loops at both ends, which makes rigging quick and easy—simply tie loops on the backing and leader butt and attach the fly line with loop-to-loop connections.

refers to it as the Twist Knot; he also lists others that have gone out of fashion for fishing, such as the Water Knot, Bowline, Jam Knot, Double Jam, Tiller Hitch, Stevedore Knot, and Figure Eight Knot. Knots come and go.

I'll spare you any tutorial on the way things used to be when it came to measuring line thickness with a micrometer to assemble lines and the leader; instead, let's look at how things are today. As I mentioned earlier, fly lines are now rated by number, lowest for light tackle (0- to 5-weight) to middleweights (5- to 9-weight) to heavier weights (from 10- to 12-weight or so),

Cortland's Tropic Plus GT Tuna Saltwater Line is a big-game line available in 13-weight for heavyweight fighters.

and then some outliers such as 13- or 14-weights for big-game ocean species such as sailfish, marlin, tuna, sharks, and the like.

My friend and my former editorial mentor at *Outdoor Life*, Vin Sparano, wrote in his book *Complete Outdoor Encyclopedia* (1998), "Fishing lines are made of a wide variety of natural and synthetic materials and as a result differ widely in their characteristics and the uses to which they can be put. No two types of lines, for example, have the same degree of elasticity, abrasion resistance, water absorption, weight, and diameter." For spinning and bait-casting, the lines today differ based on the type of fishing, and include monofilament to fluorocarbon but also braided lines, called super braids.

Let's first look at the traditional modern fishing material used as line, leader, and tippet—monofilament. One of the contemporaries of A. J. McClane was the fishing legend Joe Brooks, who wrote in his 1950 book *Salt Water Fly Fishing*, "Every time I tie on a leader I wonder what we did in the days before nylon appeared."

This material, a single strand of extruded nylon, can be tapered to form a fly-fishing leader to transfer weight into the cast going ahead of the angler and again on the backcast; a level or uniform diameter line is used as fishing line spooled on a bait-casting or spinning reel. Monofilament is strong, it's stiff enough that it resists kinking, it casts well and is easy to retrieve, and it holds knots well. It's served anglers since around World War II days when it was introduced and is the most common fishing line today. It has competition, though.

In the mid-1990s, a new type of line took the fishing world by storm, a braided line made of Dyneema or Spectra (high-modulus polyethylene gel spun through a spinneret) that had impressive tensile strength, low or almost no stretch (and therefore sensitive to fish bites or strikes), abrasion resistance, held no memory when coiled, and came in strengths with diameters thinner than monofilament. Thinner, stronger, tougher became the marketing language of the day. Because it had a fabric feel, it didn't kink and still cast well. However, its surface was slippery (compared to monofilament) and unfortunately knots were known to slip out of the line. Further, the lines were so limp they might foul your fishing by wrapping around a rod tip, causing potential rod breakage. The limpness also made for flaccid knot tying, so to speak, as wrapping loops became more difficult than when you used relatively stiff monofilament. Finally—and for many anglers the last straw—the lines were abrasive to the touch and could cut into fingers as you fished or tied knots. These factors limited the adoption of Super Braids—at least at first. One positive was that the lines generally floated, so were convenient for topwater fishing.

Over time, manufacturers improved the characteristics of the Super Braids. A primary change was to impregnate the lines with a polymer or to use a tighter braiding technique so they held together tighter than previously, and this seemed to add a little desirable stiffness to the lines. A second-generation of Super Braids is now available, and the lines are clearly here to stay. They seem to be made for spooling on bait-casting outfits, and certainly have their proponents for spinning rods. I used the lines in the mid-1990s, when they were fairly new, and was tutored in flipping and pitching by a pro while we fished a southern lake for largemouth bass. It was fun and satisfying fishing, and I liked the way the lines behaved and allowed me to get a "feel" for the plastic baits we were using as I was measuring the target distance of my flips and pitches.

These braided fishing lines have replaced Dacron (a synthetic polyester) braids in many applications—though Dacron, which is less expensive than the Super Braids, is still used as fly-line backing and for trolling in fresh and salt water.

One popular "superline" is Fireline by Berkley. The company tells us: "Berkley-branded lines are made from the highest grade Dyneema in the industry, a gel-spun polyethylene that is fifteen times stronger than steel by weight . . . Berkley superlines offer zero stretch at typical fishing loads, plus low memory and, thanks to incredibly

Stren braided Superline.

high tensile strength, remarkably thin line diameters." In the knot-tying instructions in this book, I've selected knots that work well with so-called

Cortland's Gel Spun fly-line backing is an example of a superline.

Super Braids that are mentioned by several top anglers in the sidebars in the book.

The next in the troika of today's popular fishing-line materials is fluorocarbon (polyvinylidene fluoride). Fluoro is only used as leader material because it's expensive—more expensive than mono, for sure—and it holds memory when coiled, so it is most manageable in shorter pieces when coiling isn't an issue. The same as mono, it's

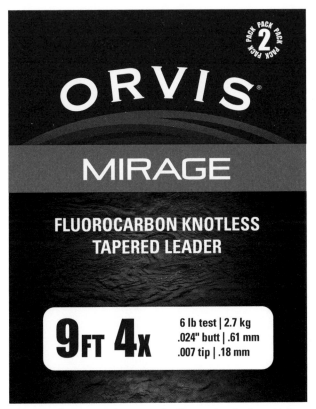

The Orvis Company makes a popular fluorocarbon leader and tippet material called Mirage.

extruded as a single piece. It actually has greater translucence than monofilament and is therefore less visible to fish underwater.

This is because fluoro has a similar refractive index to water so light passes through it. And so, because these lines are not as visible to fish, anglers can use heavier pound-test fluoro lines in fishing situations. It's also stiffer than mono, which helps casting, particularly the presentation fly cast when you're dropping the fly—the fluoro straightens out nicely as it unfurls. It absorbs no water so doesn't "weaken" while being fished, and actually sinks faster than mono and is more resistant to abrasion. It doesn't "stretch" or give as quickly as mono does, but that can play against you when a fish strikes suddenly or when you're fighting a fish and the shock absorption of mono is an advantage. When it comes to knots, fluoro must be moistened before seating the knot, otherwise you risk knot failure. This seems more crucial than when using mono—though you should moisten mono knots, too. Manufacturers have improved fluorocarbon formulations, so

Rio offers various leader and tippet materials, such as fluorocarbon material called Fluoroflex Plus tippet, tapered leaders and nylon material called Powerflex Plus, and monofilament saltwater leaders.

always read the packaging, catalogs, and website copy to learn the claimed advantages.

Without question, when I'm fishing in situations where visibility is a concern—such as the saltwater flats of the Florida Keys—I always use fluorocarbon. Years ago I was fly fishing the flats of the Keys out of the Ocean Reef Club in Key Largo. Bonefish were sporadically tailing, tipping up to feed into the coral and sand bottom with their underslung mouths, probably picking up small crabs. I had a crab fly pattern tied on, and the guide poled the boat within a longish cast of a tailing bonefish. I fired away and came up short. That's when I experienced a benefit of the fluorocarbon leader and tippet I was using: The diameter of the fluoro was smaller than six- or eight-pound-test monofilament, so my leader, tippet, and fly entered the water with nary a ripple. I didn't disturb the fish; it kept on tailing. So I picked up the fly and with a quick-snap double-haul, dropped the fly again about three feet farther out than my first cast. The "plop" of my fly striking the surface got the fish's attention, and its tail turned like a sail tacking. I made one slow and short strip of fly line and then came tight to my first bonefish. After a few thrusting runs to deep water, the fish began to tire; I slid out of the boat and held steady pressure. I brought the fish in to me as it circled, closer and closer as I reeled in line. It was a nice bone. My knots held. It was an exciting day for me in Key Largo. I thought about Curtis Point not far away on the southeast end of Old Rhodes Key, where I had once fished with Capt. Bill Curtis, the longtime fishing guide who reportedly developed the poling platform on a flats skiff and for whom the point was named.

At another occasion, on the coast of the Yucatan in Mexico, the guide poled the boat along a shore-line near a *boca* as we looked for snook—*robalo,* the guide Lemus said. I had just completed tying on a section of twenty-pound fluorocarbon as a shock tippet to guard against a snook's razor-sharp gill plates. I used a three-turn Double Clinch Knot to tie on the fly. In the wave wash, I saw what appeared to be sunken piece of driftwood. Lemus saw it too, and he motioned for me to cast. The wind was blowing across the bow of the boat, so I turned my body to present the fly on my backcast. As I began to cast, Lemus whispered urgently, "No! No!" He tensed when I released my backcast and the streamer fly landed about a foot in front of the snook's nose. "Yah!" Lemus hissed. The snook ate and after we landed the nearly twenty-pound fish, we headed back to the lodge to deliver it to the kitchen staff. Within an hour, we were eating snook *sashimi*. Again I was using fluorocarbon, with knots that a group of anglers and I had discussed the night before at the lodge, Blood Knots in the leader and the Double Clinch to tie on the fly. Success—because I knew my knots and how to tie them correctly, under pressure.

Generally, the guidelines for fishing lines are: Super Braids (or "superlines" as Berkley calls their product) are thin for their pound-test rating, have no stretch and allow an angler to haul a fish out of heavy cover, are abrasion resistant, float or suspend near the surface, are easy to

cast, but often have surfaces that are slippery and don't hold all knots well; fluorocarbon lines are thin for their pound-test rating, are resilient and abrasion resistant, yet sensitive because you can use a smaller diameter line with the same pound-test rating as thicker mono, don't stretch as much as monofilament, are less visible underwater than monofilament, but they sink so aren't great for topwater fishing, hold knots well, but develop memory when coiled and are expensive compared to monofilament; and monofilament lines are the tried-and-true fisherman's friend that have stood the test of time and are still favored by many anglers, despite some of the tradeoffs compared to the other two types of lines. One bottom line to consider is that monofilament costs less than fluorocarbon and braids, and still gets the job done. All three lines certainly hold knots, so the choice is yours.

Nevertheless, to be a competent angler—and to achieve the enjoyment of landing fish—you need to learn to tie dependable knots in all these lines. The knots carry over from material to material, but you must take care when tightening them so the loops don't slip out of sequence, causing the knot to collapse and fail. Get a supply of these materials so you can experiment and tie the knots in this book, and others you come across that look effective for your fishing, till you've got them fixed in your muscle memory. A test I use

Orvis Superstrong Plus is a knotless, tapered monofilament leader and tippet material that the company says has greater knot strength than other leader-and-tippet materials on the market.

when I feel I've learned a knot by heart is to tie it in low-light conditions or in the dark, as if I'm fishing at night. Trust The Force, my friends—The Force being your intuitive knot knowledge.

Overhand Knot

Let's begin with a foundational knot, the knowledge of which will impel you to acquire greater knot knowledge and feed your hunger for learning knots for any fishing application and purpose.

1. Loop a piece of tippet or leader material.

2. Bring the tag end back through the loop you just formed.

3. Moisten the knot with saliva and pull both ends with equal force to tighten.

Arbor Knot

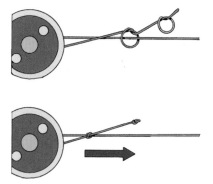

This is another foundational knot that you can use to secure backing on a fly reel or braided, monofilament, or any fishing line to the arbor of any fishing reel.

1. Bring the line around the arbor of the reel. Tie one overhand knot over the standing line, and tie another at the very end of the line, as shown here.

2. Moisten the knots and draw both knots tight, and pull on the standing line to tighten the small knot into the knot around the line, thereby jamming the knots together and securing the line.

Clinch Knot

Let's assume you reject the dynamite or hand grenade approach to fish collection—and so for most anglers, this is the first fishing knot learned: to state the obvious, you need to know how to secure your hook or lure to your fishing line, otherwise you will catch no fish. The Clinch Knot does the job, and it can be improved—as with the Improved Clinch Knot, which is the next knot listed here. You can do a lot with this knot. In fly-fishing, by tying it with a long tag end, you can tie a dropped fly for a tandem-fly rig (when it's legal), or you can tie a dropper off the hook bend of the first fly. Be deliberate when learning this knot—the confidence you get tying this one knot will help you step up to other knots necessary for other uses.

1. Pass the end of the tippet through the hook eye and form a loop with your thumb and forefinger, extending over the standing part of the tippet.

2. Wind the tag end around the standing part of the line with the thumb and forefinger of your dominant hand. Once you tie this many times, you'll develop muscle memory. On a standard knot, make five complete turns with the tag end. With lighter leaders, you can make seven or eight turns. Using

heavier-test shock tippets, only use three turns, otherwise you'll have difficulty getting the loops to set properly; three turns is enough.

3. Thread the tag end through the loop in front of the hook eye. Use saliva to lubricate the knot as you tighten it. Clip the excess tag end.

Improved Clinch Knot

Here, you'll add one further step to the Clinch Knot, improving its strength and creating the Improved Clinch.

1. Repeat step one of the Clinch, running the tag through the hook eye and making seven, five, or three wraps around the standing line (depending on the test strength of the fishing line—the stronger the line, the fewer wraps are used).

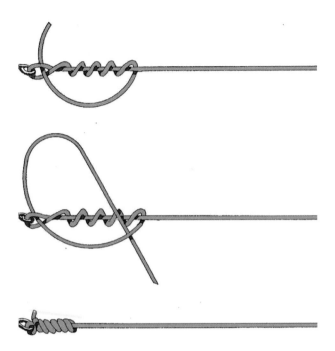

2. Bring the tag end through the loop in front of the hook eye.

3. Now, bring the tag back through the large loop formed when you passed the tag through that small loop in front of the hook eye, as seen here.

Building Leaders

with Chico Fernandez

When I was editing *Saltwater Fly Fishing* magazine in the mid-1990s and early 2000s, I became friends with columnist Chico Fernandez, who was based in Miami. Chico was a hero of mine, and I got to know him as a friendly, insightful person. He helped us out at the magazine by teaching fly-casting at the Miami Boat Show, and I enjoyed being his guest on nights out in Miami Beach. Here, he shares some advice on making leaders and the knots to use to make connections. He

makes connections—in life and in fly fishing—
easily and expertly. Very cool.

"In fly-fishing, the knots we talk about are main-
ly for the leader. And the leader is an extension
of the fly line—you're making the rest of the line
connection, and you want to make that leader
turn over just as the fly line does. One of the rules

of thumb that I advocate, and that has worked for me forever, is using a butt section that's at least 50 percent of your leader length. For example, if you have a ten-foot leader, at least five feet should be the butt section. If you have less, it won't turn over, especially in the saltwater world, but even in freshwater if you're casting with a lighter rod, like a 3-weight, you need about 50 percent. Some people adhere to the leader formula that Charles Ritz came up with in the 1930s of sixty-twenty-twenty in which sixty is the butt section and twenty and twenty are the tapered sections. If you have the right butt section, everything will turn over (when you cast). The 60 percent is a little more aggressive and will turn over a hard-bodied popper or Woolly Bugger in Alaska or a deer-hair bug. You can fluctuate between that 50 and 60 percent butt section, and that will work.

"Now, how heavy should the butt section be? Most people don't use a butt section that's heavy enough. If you use monofilament, you need to have a butt section that's thick enough and heavy enough so the fly line transmits power to the leader. It's not just diameter, it's weight. If you use common sense, you know that the weight casts the fly line. (Think of casting a weight-forward fly line, versus attempting to cast a level line, for example.) You need the proper butt section for the leader to turn over."

Chico makes an argument for using lighter fly rods, when the conditions allow, because that will reduce the weight of the fly line and leader assembly hitting the water and therefore allow you to make more delicate presentations. "Fish will feel the slap on the water of heavier leaders and lines, so lighter is better, when conditions allow," he says.

What does he use to connect leader sections? Hands down, the Blood Knot. "I don't like the Surgeon's Knot because you have to overlap the lines a lot, and if you don't pull the lines evenly, the knot doesn't set." Plus, he says, if you have to retie the leader, the Surgeon's Knot uses a lot of line and often you have to start again with fresh line, whereas you can retie Blood Knots. Further, Chico feels a Blood Knot is stronger.

And the Blood Knot doesn't create complications. "When it is set properly and trimmed, it is the most aerodynamic knot, but more importantly it doesn't catch much grass when retrieved through the water. But the Surgeon's Knot, the tags go out at angles and pick up a huge amount of grass. For these reasons, I use the Blood Knot, and I've caught everything from bonefish to bass, to sailfish, to four or five marlin, and about a million tarpon."

Chico's tip on using a Blood Knot: "You have to put more turns around the lower strength or thinner line, than around the heavier or thicker line." He recommends using a six-turn-to-four-turn configuration. However, be careful about the bulkiness of the extra turns. "You really need those extra turns going from the leader to the tippet. I don't need six-turns-to-four turns going from the butt section to the next section, way up on the leader. I need the extra strength down near the fly, from the leader to the tippet, say from twenty-pound to the twelve-pound sections that I advocate the six to four turns. It's at the end of a leader, that's the weakest link—the connection from the tippet to the next piece up. Or, for even more strength at this connection, you can tie an Improved Blood Knot. That might be a little stronger." He also mentions that you could use a Bimini to form the tippet section and tie the double line of the Bimini to the previous leader section, particularly for bigger fish such as tarpon. Finally, Chico says regardless of the type of leader, he doesn't want to fight any fish too long because that imperils the fish's chances of survival. For the terminal knot used to tie on the fly, he almost always uses a loop—usually a Duncan Loop (also called a Uni-Knot Loop).

Blood Knot

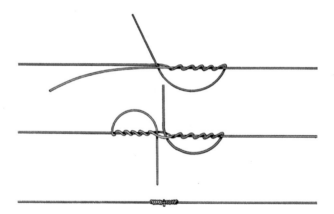

This is an elegant, utilitarian knot, often preferred by anglers for joining sections of a leader.

1. Cross two strands of monofilament so you form an X. Give yourself a break and leave about six inches of tags at the top of the X. Now "walk" the tag ends up the standing end, left and right. You'll have to focus, using some dexterity to wrap the tag ends. Use your thumb and forefinger, if needed.

2. Use seven turns for light material, five turns for regular-diameter material, and three turns for heavy stuff. After you make these turns, thread the tag ends through the loop at the X. Again, you'll need some dexterity with your fingers to do this with both tag ends.

3. Coat the knot with saliva and pull on both standing parts of line. The tag ends should extend through the loop enough so that they don't slip out when you tighten the knot. You want the wraps to be neat, tight coils or barrels, as shown here. Trim the tag ends.

Knots

with Flip Pallot

Angler's angler, spoken-word poet, television personality, flats-boat designer, all-around nice guy, and teacher by nature, Flip Pallot has acquired, through decades of fishing, an encyclopedic knowledge of what works. The following conversation occurred in a steady stream, with nary an interruption from me, simply my acknowledgements that Flip was speaking angling gospel. I got to know Flip when he wrote for *Fly Fishing in Salt Waters* magazine in the 1990s. Enjoy this, and apply it to your fishing.

"Knots all depend on what's needed for the fishing situation, and for me that's 90 percent fly fishing. Everyone has a terminal knot that they use to tie on the lure or fly, and I use two—probably the same two that 80 or 90 percent of everybody else has. I use a loop knot when I want the fly to have more action or I want the fly to sink faster. And the loop I use is the Duncan Loop. I tie the Duncan Loop in most situations where bite tippet is not involved. I tie the knot with six turns, and if I'm using stronger bite tippet I might only use three turns. The bigger and heavier the tippet, the fewer turns I'll use. By changing the number of turns, I'm able to cinch it up tight enough so that it doesn't slip and yet remains a loop.

"When I want a firm connection to the fly, I use an unimproved Clinch Knot. I usually use that with six turns, and with a heavier bite tippet, fewer turns.

"These are the knots I use each and every time I connect something. I suppose these are the knots I tie the most and therefore I have muscle memory to tie them. I don't think about it, I just tie them—they just form themselves.

"One of the other two knots that I use most frequently would be the Blood Knot, to form leaders based on a formula I have that has evolved for me over years. I also use the Blood Knot to tie each segment of my tapered leader. I understand that it's perhaps the highest-testing knot or the strongest-testing knot, but over the years I've come to realize that the leader is stronger test than the class line anyway so it's very rare to have any leader failure (using this knot) and it's a fast and efficient knot. And most of all, it doesn't require a lot of material to tie. You don't have to double the line, and figure-eight things; it just requires very little material and it can be clipped off very close and the leader can be reeled up into the rod guides if needed. The Blood Knot is involved in every leader I use, if that leader is tapered.

"Finally, the fourth knot I use and rely on most is the Snell. I use it to connect the butt section of my leader to the fly line. The Snell is very, very, very small, streamlined, and light—and it forms a terrific transition from the fly line to the butt section so all the energy from the fly line is transferred into the leader. Those are the knots that I live by, right there."

Trilene Knot

Many anglers prefer this knot for bigger or heavier lures or flies because it holds well. In fact, it often tests stronger than a Clinch Knot.

1. Start this knot the same way as you would start a Clinch Knot, but after you have brought the tippet through the hook eye, keep coming around and pass the tippet through the hook eye a second time, in the same direction as the first pass. This will

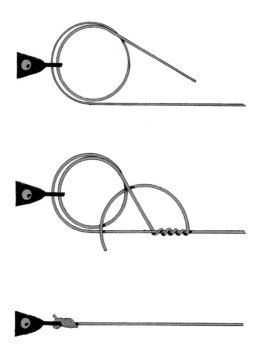

form a double loop in front of the eye as you start to make your turns around the standing part of the line. Keep this loop open with the thumb and forefinger of your left hand.

2. Wind the tag end around the standing part five times only. Bring the tag end back through the double loop in front of the eye.

3. Moisten and tighten carefully. Instead of letting go of the tag end as you would when tightening a Clinch Knot, it helps to hold the tag end tightly against the fly.

Fishing Knots

with Jimmy Houston

Thoughts on knots from the professional bass angler and television personality.

"Going back to the early 1970s, I worked for Berkley Trilene. Back then, the big fishing line was (the competitor) Stren. But Berkley hired me, Ricky Green, Tommy Martin, and Roger Moore. That was the original Trilene team (of professional anglers). They sent us out to store promotions

to talk about Trilene. One of the things they did in the early days was use line-testing machines. We affectionately named one R2-D2, because that was about the time when *Star Wars* came out. It broke line at a certain test strength, and what we had it for was to show people how breaking strength worked. That was new back then. But we also used it as a teaching tool to show people how to tie good knots. Most people tied a Clinch Knot, and it pulled through at about seventy percent. If you tied a swivel on, it would break at about 14 or 15 percent. And so we would teach people to tie a good knot."

The Trilene Knot came about, Jimmy remembers, when he and Ricky Green were fooling around during fishing promotions, trying different knots, and trying to get people to change over from Stren fishing line to Trilene—and to teach people how to tie better fishing knots. "Back then, Ricky Green and I did a lot of those store promotions. A lot of times in those days, at a promotion, we would tie thousands of knots. We tried every kind of quirky thing to tie knots, and then put it on the machine and let it break it or try to break it or pull it through. Well, Ricky Green and I actually developed the Trilene knot for those promotions. We showed it to Trilene and told them, 'Hey, this is sensational, it's a great knot.' Everyone was comparing it to the Palomar Knot. If you tie the Palomar Knot well, it's 100 percent. So we showed our knot to Trilene, and I said 'I want to call it the Jimmy Houston Knot.' And Ricky Green said, 'Well, I want to call it the Ricky Green Knot.' When we came up with it we were playing with that machine, and it wouldn't break. That's the origin of the Trilene knot. In the process of all that they didn't call it the Jimmy Houston or the Ricky Green knot, they called it the Trilene Knot, which is how it's known today. This was probably the late 1970s.

"Back in the seventies and eighties, people didn't know how to tie fishing knots. It's no different now. We go to kids' fishing derbies to teach, we work them all around the country."

Eventually, Jimmy did develop a knot known as the Jimmy Houston Knot. "I took a Clinch Knot and doubled that, and was playing around with that, a double Improved Clinch—doubling the line and running through the eye of the lure and then wrapping four times around the double line. This was more or less killing time at these promotions, so I called this one the Jimmy Houston Knot, and this was a pure 100 percent knot, in monofilament or braid. You can break a lure off and go and retrieve that lure and you'll see the line broke but not the knot. The only time you can make that knot fail is if you cinch it down wrong and the line cuts itself. What it really is, is a Double Improved Clinch. That goes back now about forty years. We got it down to where four wraps would hold it. If I'm fishing a plastic worm, I leave the tags long because they will tuck inside the worm and hold the worm straight. People who watch us on TV know that as the Jimmy Houston Knot.

"Knots are an integral part of fishing. We taught a lot of people how to tie knots, including how to tie the Jimmy Houston Knot—and the cool thing, that knot is a 100 percent knot in mono, fluorocarbon, or braid," Jimmy concludes.

Albright Knot

In saltwater fishing, you'll often need to connect lines of different diameters; sometimes, the materials are different, such as when you join monofilament to fluorocarbon. You'll find the Albright Knot most useful for joining these different lines, particularly when building leaders for big-game species (usually in saltwater fishing), or attaching a fly line to its backing.

1. Make a loop in the tag end of the heavier leader material, overlapping with the line with the tag end a couple inches. Pass the lighter material through this loop and pinch it against the heavier material. Give yourself a couple inches of material to work with.

2. Wrap the lighter material over the doubled section of heavier material, working toward the loop. You want about ten to twelve turns. (I recommend using twelve.) On the same side that you entered the loop, pass the lighter material back through the loop, as shown here.

3. Pull on the standing parts of the lighter material and the heavier material—pull steadily, don't rush. Allow the coils to form toward the end of the loop. Pull the tag end of the

lighter material to seat the coils. Next, pull steadily on the standing part of the lighter material, coaxing the coils to the end of the loop in the heavier material. Using pliers, pull the tag end of the lighter line, hard. Pull equally on the light standing line and heavy tag to secure the knot. Trim the tag ends.

Note: In the classic knot-tying book *Practical Fishing Knots II*, the authors Mark Sosin and Lefty Kreh recommend using a finishing knot to lock the tag end of the lighter line of the Albright in place, the same way you would lock the Bimini Twist (see steps 3 and 4 of the Bimini on page 82).

Fishing the Albright Knot
(Also called the Albright Special)
with Phil Monahan

Credit: Sandy Hays

Phil is the former editor of *American Angler* magazine and a former fishing guide in Alaska and Montana. Now the editor of the Orvis Fly Fishing blog, he enjoys fishing the small streams near his home in southern Vermont and traveling across the country reporting on fly-fishing developments. He and I edited fly-fishing magazines during the 1990s, when "how-to" was important to the readership, long before you could find instruction on much of the sport through YouTube.

"The Albright Knot is one of my favorite knots—strangely, because it is so complicated to tie. The trend in knots is to create the strongest knots with as few moves as possible and to try to get the smallest knot possible. I remember when I was first starting to fly fish and I saw an illustration for the Albright Knot that featured ten to twelve loops—that's a lot of loops! It was super intimidating at first, and I think I spent a lot of time and quite a bit of backing perfecting it. But when it does come together, it's actually a very attractive knot. It has that slim, tight profile. When you get all of those wraps to lie perfectly one next to the other, and you tug as hard as you can and you can't make anything budge, it's satisfying. And because it's hidden inside your reel, you never see it. If you're fishing quite a bit, you will retie your Blood Knots, but the Albright Knot is something you don't want to worry about. You want to know you have ten to twelve wraps connecting that thing and there's no way it's going to fail you. The process is very satisfying: to get everything to work perfectly in a somewhat complicated knot, to pull it tight, and have everything seat perfectly, and be able to clip those tag ends really close."

Phil doesn't feel he needs to use super glue to make the knot stronger: Once it's tied, it's tied. "Putting super glue on it is gilding the lily. It's a knot, so it's supposed to hold. Let's not complicate it." He uses the Albright exclusively to attach his fly line to the backing on the reel, as many fly fishers do. Anglers report using the knot to join lines of different diameters, or monofilament or fluorocarbon to braided lines, often in big-game saltwater applications.

Phil reminds me he used to tie my Albright Knots when we worked together while I edited *Saltwater Fly Fishing* and he edited *American Angler*. (Okay, I suppose he did tie one or two for me.) "When I was a fishing guide in Alaska, I got a lot of knot practice back in the day. To get me from the fly to the backing on my reel, I feel like it should go Clinch Knot, Blood Knot, Perfection Loop, Albright Knot. It's also cool to tie a knot named after (famous fishing guide) Jimmie Albright."

Albright was a saltwater pioneer who guided countless anglers and many celebrities in the Florida Keys, including baseball legend Ted Williams. In the *New York Times* obituary when Albright died in 1998, Richard Stanczyk of Bud 'n' Mary's Marina in Islamorada is quoted as saying: "Jimmie and Ted were a lot alike. Both of them were competitive, expert, tough, and cantankerous. Jimmie had a great sense of humor, but he was also very dedicated and disciplined. He took his guiding seriously, and helped make the industry a legitimate profession." Albright advanced the sport in many ways; he is also credited with developing the Blood Knot.

Keep the faith, Phil.

Bimini Twist

Doubling your class tippet is insurance when fighting big, hard-fighting fish. International Game Fish Association (IGFA) regulations allow you to use this insurance when you're fishing for records, thereby creating a 100 percent connection between your class tippet and shock or bite tippet. How cool is that? But you'll have to master this knot to do so. If you ever fish for record catches, and plan to submit a record for IGFA consideration, you'll want a Bimini in your leader configuration.

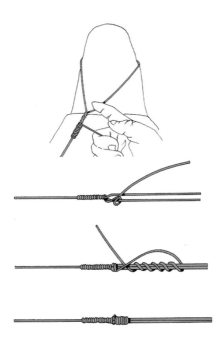

1. Make a loop with your class-tippet material, put a hand into the loop, and twirl it twenty or thirty times. Now place the loop around something stationary—over your knee (as shown here), or some anglers place the loop over a doorknob. Make sure the now-twisted loop is closed tight. While you have the

loop over your knee or a doorknob, place your forefinger at the Y formed where the loop meets the twists. Slowly release the tag end as you push a finger against the fork of the Y. What you're doing is letting the tag end roll over the twists. It's pretty cool! Don't let the coils bunch up or overwrap; it helps to slightly elevate the tag end as you push that index finger. When you have a neat group of coils, secure the knot by making a half-hitch in the Y.

2. Do it again on the other side. Now do it a third time around both sides.

3. Make a Clinch Knot setup around the legs, winding the tag end five times around the doubled line and tighten that, slowly and evenly. Pull the tag end with pliers to make sure the knot is tight and that it seats properly. Make an overhand knot to secure the whole thing.

4. The result is a double line on one end and single line on the other. This is commonly used as the class tippet connection in a

leader, especially when you're fishing for record catches—the Bimini is the leader section you would submit to a record organization to have a record catch certified. The rules from the International Game Fish Association (IGFA) state: "Fly rod applications must include the entire leader still attached to the fly. All other records must include 50 feet of the main line still attached to the double line and/or leader." For more info, go to igfa.org.

Huffnagle Knot

When you need to employ a Bimini Twist as a class tippet (kind of a middle transitional section, before the business end of the bite or shock tippet), joining it to a heavy bite or shock tippet (usually for saltwater fishing), give the Huffnagle Knot a try.

1. Make an overhand knot in the heavy leader material, a couple inches from the end. Draw this knot up to form a figure eight, and place

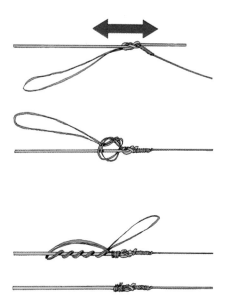

the loop end of the Bimini Twist through the loop, and then back around through the other loop, as shown here. Pull the heavy leader material tight, closing the knot. You joined the two lines, now you finish the knot. Trim the heavy tag end.

2. Knot the loop of the Bimini around the heavy leader material, as shown above.

3. Now use the loop of the Bimini, looping it around the heavy leader material five times (like you did when finishing the Bimini). Pull the tag end and coax the coils of the resulting knot into an even, though unruly, bunch—slowly and deliberately.

4. Pull on the loop tag end and the heavy (shock) tippet to tighten. Trim the tag.

Orvis Knot

Use this knot for fresh or saltwater applications. See the interview below with Tom Rosenbauer of Orvis to learn more about the history of this knot.

1. Pass the tippet through the eye of the lure or fly, coming up from the bottom, and make a loop, as shown here.
2. Bring the tag around the standing line, making another loop.

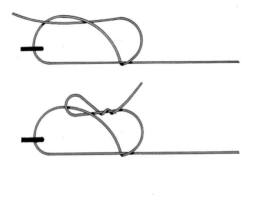

3. Make two turns around the new loop.

4. Apply some saliva and pull the fly and the tag end, to tighten against the hook eye. Trim the excess tag.

Note: The Orvis Company CEO Perk Perkins made this knot even more useful with a version called the Orvis Tippet Knot. You use the same engineering for both knots, only this one joins lines (whereas the other secures the fly or lure hook). Start this knot by overlapping tippet and leader lines by six to eight inches. Form a loop as you did above, and then make a second loop and bring the tag ends through that loop a couple times, as you did above. Moisten the knot, pinch the tag ends on the standing line, and draw the knot tight, pulling evenly. Clip the tag ends.

About the Orvis Knot

with Tom Rosenbauer

For more than forty years, Tom Rosenbauer has worked in a variety of capacities for Vermont's Orvis Company, the country's oldest hunting and fishing mail-order company founded in 1856. He has also written some of the most instructive books to date on fly fishing. His book, *The Orvis Guide to Fly Fishing*, is one of the most accessible introductions to the sport published in the modern era. I've had some superb days fishing with Tom, including time spent with him and Capt. Tony Biski on the flats of Monomoy Island off the coast

of Cape Cod and with Tom on the Battenkill in Vermont.

"In the 1990s, Orvis had a contest where people could submit their own knots. We had all the knots tested on an Instron (knot testing machine) and a guy name Larry Becker submitted this knot, which some people claimed was another knot, but the truth was nobody had ever seen it anywhere. It's a very simple knot to tie. Perk and Dave Perkins (the CEO and vice chairman of Orvis, respectively) are very good anglers and they use it exclusively to tie on a fly.

"One of the biggest benefits of this knot is that it's consistent. If you've ever been involved with knot tests—and I have been—you realize that most of the knots people use are very inconsistent. For instance, a Clinch Knot or an Improved Clinch Knot may be close to 95 percent, if tied perfectly. But we found if you take a really good knot tier, and he or she ties ten knots, you're going to find 20 or 30 percent variation in the breaking strength. Inconsistency in knots is a real issue and there doesn't seem to be a way around

it. The Orvis Knot is a really consistent knot, and it's so easy that it's tough to tie it improperly. And it's a really strong knot and it's clean. When he first saw it, Perk Perkins said, 'Aw, that's a cool knot.' He came up with a way to use the same knot to join two pieces of tippet materials—the Orvis Tippet Knot."

Surgeon's Knot

1. You're joining two pieces of line with this knot, so begin by overlapping the tag ends by four to six inches. Make an overhand knot loop in the overlapped line and pinch the junction of the loop with your thumb and forefinger.

2. Make another overhand knot with the doubled line. Moisten this connection with saliva—I usually pop the whole thing in my mouth—which will help secure it when you pull tight.

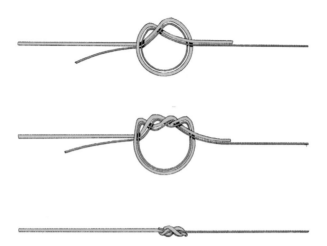

3. Hold the heavy and light line and pull quickly and tightly. Be firm, be decisive! Trim the tag ends.

Surgeon's Loop

The Surgeon's Loop is a double overhand knot that forms a loop. It's a little bulky when using heavier material, but it's effective. The Perfection Loop is an alternative for many anglers.

1. Form a loop and overlap the tag end with the standing leader for about six inches.
2. Make an overhand knot in the doubled section and pass the single loop through the double loop you have just formed. Don't jump the gun and tighten—yet.

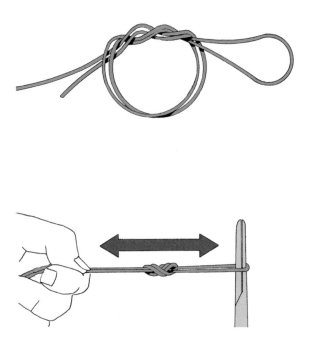

3. Make another turn of the single loop through the doubled loop. In practice, this is simply two overhand knots on top of one another. As always, pull tight and trim the tag.

Perfection Loop

As the name implies, this loop knot allows you to achieve a perfect loop in line with the standing section of the leader.

1. Start by making a loop, and adjust the tag end so it extends at a right angle. You'll need a second, smaller loop in front of the first one. Do this by bringing the tag end around the first loop, as shown here.

2. Pass the tag between the two loops. It should end up pointing at a right angle to the standing section of the line. Pinch it in place with your thumb. Pull the second loop through the first. Don't let the tag end stray or creep. The loop will tighten when you pull the second loop straight above the standing part of the leader. Moisten.

3. Here's the finished loop—now clip the tag.

Double Figure Eight Loop Knot

1. You'll need a good amount of excess line at the tag end to tie this knot. Tie a double overhand knot in the fishing line. Thread the tag end of the line through the hook eye. Adjust the overhand knot so it lays sideways, revealing the figure eight that gives the knot its name.

2. Bring the tag end up through the first and second loops of the double overhand knot (as shown here). Pull the tag through.

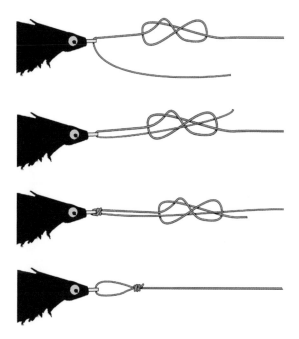

3. Tighten that first knot connection at the hook eye. Bring the tag end around the standing line two times to make another double overhand knot. Now you have the second figure eight, made by the second double overhand knot. Bring the tag end through the second loop, as shown here.

4. Moisten the knots. Pull both hook bend and the standing line to slide up the first knot, joining the knots together to form the loop of the hook eye. Clip the excess.

About the Double Figure Eight Loop Knot

with Jerry Gibbs

When you've been at the forefront of fishing writing for a couple decades, as was Jerry Gibbs while serving as Fishing Editor for *Outdoor Life* magazine till the mid-2000s (taking up that mantle in the 1970s following the great Joe Brooks), you tend to learn a knot or two—or hundreds. Jerry did exemplary work for *OL* during those decades, and while I was his editor there in the

early 1990s, I'm proud to say we became friends. Interestingly, we've hunted birds together more than we've fished, but I've learned lots from Jerry through the years. I asked him about fishing knots, and he came up with a beautiful recommendation—the Double Figure Eight Loop Knot. The knot Jerry describes here in his own words is similar to the Homer Rhode Loop Knot (included in this book), only you'll double up the overhand knots each time, before securing the loop in place.

"I figure that with inherently less flexible heavier tippets, any little extra you can give to add movement to your fly is a good thing. Thus a loop knot is a good thing. That said, back in the day, pioneering Florida Keys guide Nat Ragland often went to great effort of snelling many of his streamers (aided by the front-end shank space of classic Florida Keys–style tarpon flies) feeling he got better hook sets. I still like a loop connection and, of course, want one that's strong, easy to tie, and, with flies, facilitates a straight swim. I've used a Homer Rhode Loop Knot, which is really simple to tie but sometimes results in a slight offset or kink that discourages a straight fly swim. The Uni is really awful to cinch up tight on a heavy tippet.

"In the end, I discovered the Double Figure Eight, popularized by Capt. Steve Huff of South Florida, perhaps the most innovative and insightful angler and guide living today. This knot answered all my criteria. Of course, you can use it with a hard-bodied lure, soft plastic, or bait hook. It's not confined only to those eighty-pound-test mono tippets; I've used it down to thirty-pound test. After that, I might switch off to a Non-slip Mono Loop as in, say, a twenty-pound-test or lighter tippet, because with that lighter material there's no need to drop your hook over an object—hard or short piece of rope tied into a loop—to snug up the Figure Eight, which is something I always do working with heavier tippet. On trips where it's impractical to carry one of those fly-leader stretchers, I've used the knot to quickly tie up a batch of flies to forty- and sixty-pound test tippet, coiled the tippet and the rest of the leader, and stowed them in zippered plastic bags. Taking them out for use, a little hand stretching and everything was fine—and my flies swam straight."

Fish-N-Fool Knot

This knot was a winner on the video series *Knot Wars,* which pitted well-known knots against each other on a knot-testing machine to prove which was strongest.

1. Thread the tag end up through the hook eye, twice, forming a double loop around the hook eye. Give yourself a length of about eight to ten inches of tag section.

2. Make a loop with the tag end, holding the loop nearest the hook eye between your fin-

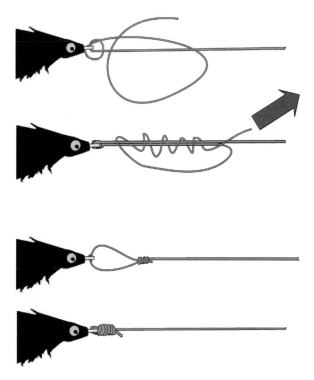

gers. Wrap the tag end over and up around the top doubled line five to seven times.

3. Moisten the knot and pull the tag end and the hook at the same time to cinch the knot. The loop shown above is for illustration pur-

poses: when you tighten it, the knot's barrel wraps will secure against the hook eye.

4. This is how the finished knot should sit. Clip the excess tag.

Conventional Tackle Knots
with Steve Pennaz

Steve was the longtime editor of *North American Fisherman* magazine, the publication of the North American Fishing Club, for which he was also executive director. (Full disclosure: I worked with Steve and another excellent editor named Kurt Beckstrom at the magazine in 1995.) He also was the host of several fishing television shows through the years, and he oversaw and hosted the series *Knot Wars*, which pitted two knots tied

with braided, monofilament, and fluorocarbon line on a knot-testing machine to prove which was stronger with each line type. *Knot Wars* became a top paid sports app when it was launched in 2010. The knots Steve talks about here come out of the testing in the *Knot Wars* competition. (Find videos online by searching "Knot Wars.")

"I live in the North Country (in Minnesota) and we do a lot of fishing at night and in the winter when your hands are so cold it's hard to tie a knot, so I like to use knots I can tie essentially without light—knots that are easy to tie. The Improved Clinch has been around for many, many years and millions of anglers use it because it's strong and effective. But one of the knots that came out of *Knot Wars* is called the Fish-N-Fool Knot; it's basically a modified Uni Knot. It goes through the hook eye twice and wraps up. What I like about this knot is that I can tie it with numb hands. And it did win *Knot Wars*, I think it was the first year of the competition, as the strongest knot, beating the Palomar and others. That knot performed very well on all three types of lines.

"I've always struggled with the leader-to-line connection. I've been using the Uni-to-Uni for many years, it's a decent knot, but it's not the strongest. I know a lot of guys like to tie the Blood Knot, but for some reason that knot and I just don't get along real well. I heard from some guys north of the border (in Canada) about a knot called the Bob Foran Knot. You can go online and find instructions for tying it. The guys I talk to, and the guys who I trust, are becoming bigger and bigger fans of it." Steve says he's had the Uni-to-Uni fail so he's looking for a replacement, and the Bob Foran Knot might be it.

"The lines are so good today, and the equipment has become so good, I think anglers have become so much better than even a generation ago, in terms of efficiency and effectiveness and overall skill. With catch-and-release, anglers are catching more and bigger fish. And I think they're becoming more effective at landing giant fish, too. Knot failure is not a thing of the past, but people are much better and better equipped to push tackle to the limits. Frankly, in freshwater there are very few species that allow you to push the limits of tackle. Basically, you're equipped for the situation. Braided lines are still an issue for some anglers because you cannot use knots with braids that you'd use with other fishing lines. The braids are too slippery for knots like the Improved Clinch, the knots will slip right out. As long as you're using the right knot for the line, I think you'll be in good shape.

"Anglers will benefit from taking the time to practice knot tying—if you're watching TV, take the time and practice tying knots. If you really practice and study the knots, as you work on them, you'll get there. The cinching process of a knot makes an absolute, massive difference in its overall strength."

Braided Knot

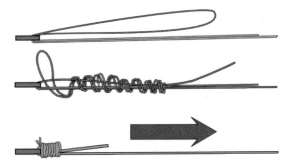

This knot is a triple threat, proving effective on braided superlines, monofilaments, and fluorocarbons.

1. Double over the braided line and run the loop through the hook eye.
2. Bring a section of doubled line back over the standing line and loop it around the standing line eight to ten times.
3. Run the loop between the hook eye and the first coil, and tighten it slowly and carefully. Clip the double line and the tag.

Crawford Knot

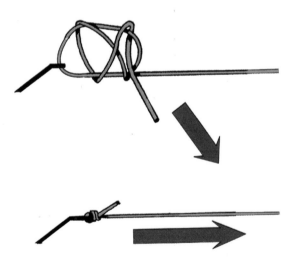

1. Holding the hook shank with your left hand, run the tag end through the hook eye and bring the end back underneath and around the standing line. Pass the tag end in front of the loop and back around through the loop, as shown here. Moisten the knot with saliva and pull the tag end down.

2. Now firmly hold the hook and pull the tag end to tighten the loop of line in the finished knot, against the hook eye. Clip the excess.

Dropper Loop

When you want to fish a tandem rig and have one fly extending off the leader and another on the terminal end, use this knot; you can tie another tippet section to this loop to drop a lure or fly off it.

1. Make a loop in the line.
2. Wind the tag end back through the loop five or six times. Holding the connection so the loop is standing up, pull the middle of the big

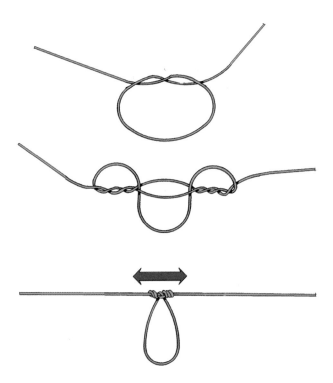

loop down through the wraps you created, as shown here. This forms the loop.

3. Moisten the wraps with saliva and pull the two ends of the line, securing the loop in place. You don't have to pull on the loop at

all; the wraps tighten the loop in place. There are similarities here to how a Blood Knot is formed.

Duncan Knot/Loop or Uni-Knot

1. Bring the tag end through the hook eye (or around a reel's arbor). At the end closest to the hook eye or the reel, begin wrapping the tag around the standing line. Do this four or five times, each time passing the tag end through the bottom loop.

2. Bring the tag one final time through the bottom loop, and then pull the tag to tighten the knot, as shown here.

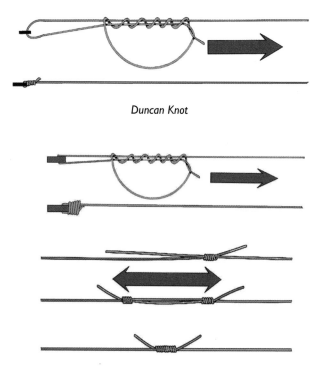

Duncan Knot

Uni-Knot

Note: You can tighten this knot to form a loop, or join two sections of line with a Uni-to-Uni using the knot shown here and drawing together the knots into one strong connection.

Using the Duncan Loop (a.k.a. Uni-Knot)

by Tom Keer

It would figure that one of my favorite knots has three different names. The original name for the multiple overhand knot was the Gallows Knot, and it was first published in 1944. Later, in the early 1960s, a man named Norman Duncan twisted it up, and did so without knowing that what he thought was his knot had already been written about. That was the knot I learned to tie, and I knew it as the Duncan Loop. About a decade

later in the 1970s, Vic Dunaway, a fishing editor from Florida, wrote about the Duncan Loop and referred to it as the Uni-Knot. Call it what you will, it's still the same great knot. And these days, the Uni-Knot may be more fitting. Why? It's universal, in many regards. The knot ties well with monofilament, fluorocarbon, and braided line. It is equally useful across all fishing disciplines. Use it when fishing with live bait; tie on a plug, spinner, or spoon; or use it with a variety of flies.

The Duncan Loop (also called the Uni-Knot) is useful for many other applications, too. Use the Duncan Loop instead of an Arbor Knot to attach line to a reel arbor. Use the same knot when attaching a leader to a hook, a swivel, or a three-way rig. This MVK (Most Valuable Knot) is strong and tests out at more than 95 percent breaking strength. The benefit is that it holds up under the steady pressure of a sounding and running fish, as well as the pounding jerks associated with a jumping, tugging fish. No matter how your favorite species fights, the Duncan Loop provides an edge. But here's what I like best, and perhaps this is why it's known as both the Duncan Loop and the Uni-Knot—it's a loop knot as well as a fixed knot. Seat the Duncan Loop a quarter of an inch above your fly or bait, and it'll function as a loop. Streamer and nymph flyfishermen, big fly saltwater anglers, and live bait anglers love the additional natural movement that comes from a loop knot. When a fish hits, the Duncan Loop slides until it snugs down to the hook eye. Then it miraculously transforms into a fixed knot. If you're tying on a plug, a soft plastic, or a stickbait, you can always seat the knot to the hook eye. Three names for one knot with universal applications—you've gotta love it.

Figure Eight Knot

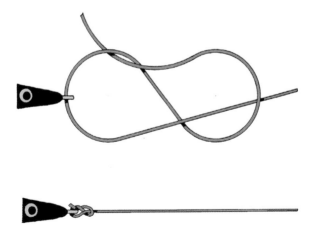

1. Bring the tag end through the hook eye, and bring it around to form a figure eight, as shown here.

2. Tighten the knot against the hook eye, and clip the tag end.

Flower Knot

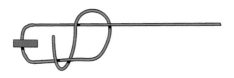

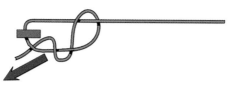

1. Bring the tag end through the hook eye and then loop it up and over the standing line.
2. Bring the tag inside the loop, and then back past the outside of the loop, as shown here.
3. Moisten, tighten the knot, and clip the tag.

Fishing the Flower Knot

with Peter Corbin

Credit: Graham Kenan Hegamyer.

Recommended by fine artist, sportsman, and master angler Peter Corbin of Shooter's Hill in Millbrook, New York—also a longtime friend.

The Flower Knot is a dependable replacement for a Clinch Knot, Peter Corbin says. However, Corbin also warns it can pull out if it's not tied properly: "I think what happens is, the last tag on the pull-through will just be a curlicue, because it has to reverse to tighten up properly. The knot is really quick—it's an overhand knot, and then the tag goes back through the other way to complete it. It's simple. As I get older, and I have to change my glasses or whatever when tying a knot, I can always do this one. My hunting partner Jim Kline showed it to me, and initially I did have a little trouble keeping clear which way I was coming with the tag after I did the first overhand; I had to make sure I was wrapping around the right part of the line. When I was up in Canada (Atlantic salmon fishing) and Sam Dempster (a guide on the Hawke River in Canada) showed me the knot, he said so many people are tying it because it's easier than the Clinch Knot. I can't claim any originality on this, I can only say that it works. Supposedly, it's stronger than a clinch, too. Between this, a Perfection Loop, and a Uni-Knot, and I don't have to clutter up my mind with anything else—you can tie just about anything."

Corbin says he uses the Uni-Knot to join lines of different diameters—a leader butt to a leader midsection, for example—and he's had the lighter line break, possibly from the friction created when tightening the knot. Corbin shares a tip: joining mono to braided backing (or mono to a section of braided line), he uses six turns around the braid to complete the Uni-Knot.

George Harvey
Dry Fly Knot

If you love trout, you should know the name George Harvey. His obituary reads: "Having organized what is believed to be the first college angling course in the US, Mr. Harvey became known as the Dean of American Fly Fishing." He was a legendary angler, yes, but he was also a legendary teacher who indoctrinated countless anglers into fly fishing through his coursework at Penn State. We honor the man and his legacy by including this knot.

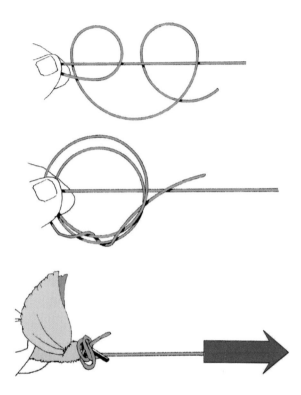

1. Bring the tag end through the hook eye, and loop the line twice around the standing line, forming two circles.

2. Bring the tag end around the loops, pinch the loops with your fingers, and bring the tag

end over and around, as shown here, exiting behind the loops.

3. Draw the knot tight and clip the tag. (And remember to say, "Thank you, Professor Harvey" when you land a fish using this knot.)

Improved Turle Knot

1. Run the tag end through the hook eye and form a loop of line (shown here looped around the head of the fly).
2. Form another loop with the tag, forward of the fly or lure, and bring the tag through that three times.
3. Pull the knot tight, coaxing the small loop over the head of the fly or lure, into position against the hook eye.

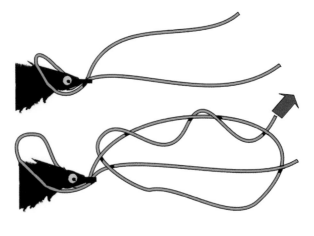

Fishing the Improved Turle Knot

by Tom Keer

Ever watch a dry fly with a down-turned ring eye ride nose-down in the surface film? Or have you seen a salmon fly with an up-turned ring eye ride whopper-jawed? I have, and I was the one who tied them on the line. Let me tell you this from experience: no self-respecting trout or salmon will hit a fly looking like that. At least they've never hit mine. Our modern-day problem was solved a long time ago thanks to a nineteenth century Brit, Major William Greer Turle. While this gentleman did not invent the knot named after him, he did popularize it. Why? To solve the same problem you and I face with nose-down riding flies.

The Improved Turle Knot is a loop tied and seated behind the ring eye. A loop, which is essentially a lasso, is tied at the end so that when the knot is seated it retracts to secure against the head of the fly. Because the knot is attached to the head, dry flies ride perfectly on the surface. Instead of having a pressure point where the knot meets the hook ring, the lasso approach spreads out pressure points, thereby offering 95 percent breaking strength. Since the monofilament passes through the ring there is a degree of movement in the fly, too. It's not a lot, but it's more than a fixed knot will allow. To me, the biggest point is that the leader and the hook shank are directly in line. And that is why your dry fly floats exactly where it was designed to ride: high on the surface or directly in the surface film.

Nail Knot

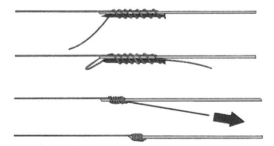

Use a small nail—hence the knot's name, used in this style of tying as popularized by the great Joe Brooks of *Outdoor Life,* but known to be developed by Florida Keys fishing guide Jimmie Albright—as the foundation around which to form this knot.

1. Make seven wraps around the line and the nail, as shown here.
2. Bring the tag end back through the gap provided by the nail, again as shown here.
3. Withdraw the nail and pull the tag end of the line. Make sure the wraps stay lined up neatly, and don't bunch up. Bunched wraps can cause knot failure.
4. Here's the finished knot with the tag clipped. Some anglers add super glue (cyanoacrylate adhesive) over the wraps to ensure that they don't separate.

Needle Nail Knot

This is a similar premise to the Nail Knot, only now you use a needle to "sow" your leader into the fly line. This is a great way to attach a leader butt section to the fly line.

1. Start by threading the line into the center of the fly line.
2. Wrap the line around the fly line, using the needle as a base, as you would a Nail Knot.

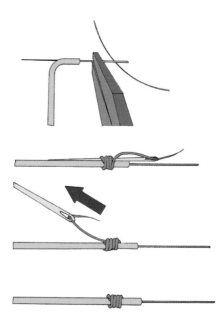

Pull the tag end under the knot wraps, using the needle as your aid.

3. Tie off and clip the tag, making sure the wraps are lined up properly and not bunched.

Double Nail-Knot Loop

1. Use the Nail Knot to secure the heavier line or fly line into a loop. Start by doubling over the heavier line. Tie a Nail Knot using a needle or other straight object.
2. Here's the first finished Nail Knot.
3. Now secure the loop with a second Nail Knot. Again, some anglers coat the Nail Knots with super glue or silicone. Your call on that.

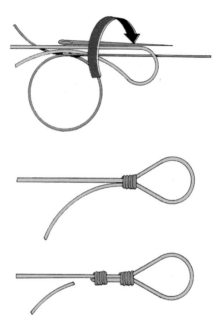

Whipped Loop

A convenient way to form a loop at the end of the fly line (the forward end for attaching the leader, the back end for using a loop-to-loop connection for the reel's backing) is simply whipping a loop using fly-tying thread. You can then attach the leader with a loop-to-loop connection. (Some fly-line manufacturers make fly lines with loops at the ends, saving us the trouble.)

1. Start by forming a loop in the fly line and wrapping fly-tying thread many times around

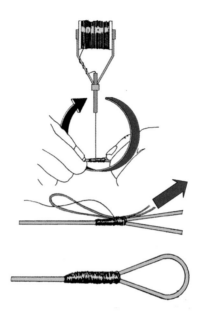

the tag end of the fly line to secure the loop in place. (You can peel off the fly-line coating if you'd prefer and make a loop with the exposed braided line underneath—your choice.)

2. Lay a short loop section of heavy monofilament over the thread wraps and make about ten more thread wraps over the mono. Run

the thread through the mono loop and with-draw it from under the thread wraps, making a "trap wrap" and securing the thread.

3. This is the slightly tapered Whipped Loop. Some anglers coat the thread with super glue or other fixative to ensure the loop won't pull out. Your choice.

Homer Rhode Loop Knot

This is an excellent utilitarian loop knot for when you want to impart more action to a lure or a fly. The man for whom the knot is named, Homer Rhode Jr., was a fly-rod pioneer in South Florida and the Everglades in the mid-twentieth century. He originated the Homer Rhode Jr. Tarpon Streamer (similar in design to the tarpon Seaducer popularized by Chico Fernandez) and the Homer Rhode Jr. Tarpon Bucktail, which were both featured in *Streamer Fly Tying and Fishing* by Joseph D.

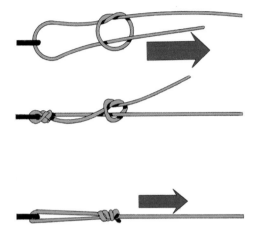

Bates Jr. Rhodes wrote to Bates, and is quoted in the book, "You'll note that all of my neck hackle and saddle hackle flies are tied with very heavy collars." He also wrote: "When I dress flies on offset hooks I removed about 90 percent of the offset, which seems to give the best results in hooking and holding fish." A little classic fishing tip from an early saltwater master.

1. Make an overhand knot a couple inches from the end of the line. Bring the tag end

through the hook eye, and back through the overhand loop, as shown here.

2. Draw up this knot against the hook eye— loosely. Make another overhand knot around the standing line.

3. Moisten the knots and pull the lure or fly by the hook bend, causing the first overhand knot to jam up against the second. Clip the tag end.

Non-slip Mono Loop Knot

Déjà vu? Yes—you start this knot the same as you did the Homer Rhode Loop.

1. Make an overhand knot in the line and pass the tag end through the hook eye, bringing the tag back through the overhand knot, as seen here. Now get Clinch knotty—wrap the tag around the standing line five time, as seen here. Use four turns for line heavier than forty-pound-test.

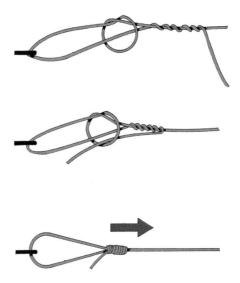

2. Now reverse yourself—bring the tag back through the overhand knot loop, on the same side you did previously.

3. Tighten by pulling the tag end, with pliers if you have them. Then pull the lure or fly by the hook bend to seat the knot as you hold the standing line, and you should have your loop—Non-slip, just as intended.

Palomar Knot

This knot has lots of history as a fisherman's helper, but recently has been maligned as it doesn't always test out at 100 percent on knot machines. When you tie it right, thought, the Palomar won't let you down.

1. Begin by doubling the line, threading it through the hook eye, giving yourself enough length, and forming an overhand knot, as shown here.

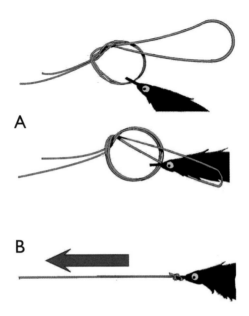

A

B

2. Bring the fly or lure through the knot (or bring the loop over the fly or lure).

3. Pull the standing line and the fly or lure by the hook bend to seat the knot, and clip the tag end.

Slim Beauty

While editing *Saltwater Fly Fishing* magazine, I got to know Capt. Tom Rowland, and he later helped develop this knot; he's also a creative fly tier. Rowland guided in the Rocky Mountains and later in Key West, Florida, and was known as a hard-working, no-nonsense angler. He now produces television shows, and you can find out more about this knot (including an excellent video on tying it) at www.saltwaterexperience.com. He tells the story at the website about how this knot

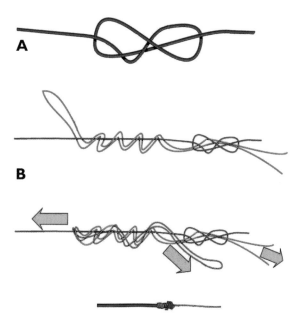

A

B

was named—not for the profile of the knot, but in a humorous reference to the nickname a waitress gave him one night at a Cuban restaurant, Slim Beauty.

1. Tie a double figure eight in the leader, and rotate the knot at this stage so the concave

loops curve up, making it easier to complete this knot.

2. Double your other leader material, and thread the doubled loop in and out, through the two loops of the figure eight, as shown here. Draw the figure eight a little tighter—but not too tight. The next step is to wrap the joining leader material five times up the other leader material (A).

3. Now wrap the doubled line four times back to the overhand knot connection, threading it through the first loop you made (B).

4. Pull tight, slowly and deliberately securing the knot, and trim the tag ends. This is what the finished knot should look like.

Fishing the Slim Beauty

with Terry Gibson

Terry Gibson has worked at magazines including *Saltwater Fly Fishing*, *Florida Sportsman*, and *Outdoor Life*, and also has worked tirelessly on conservation issues. He lives in Florida and often spends part of the year in Wyoming, so he fishes in both salt and fresh water.

"When I was working at *Florida Sportsman* magazine, Jeff Weakley, editor, showed me how to tie this knot. He showed it to me in the context of tying it so you could wind it through the guides

of a conventional offshore rod. It's a really great knot to tie, when you're joining materials for a leader, or in fly fishing, tying the leader to the tippet. It's really strong; I've never had one break that I've tied right. I've used it for tarpon leaders, but primarily I've used it for offshore fishing—trolling and kite fishing, that sort of thing. It's nice for kite fishing in a tournament because once you reel the leader into the rod tip, it's an official release. With any kind of guide on a rod—roller guides or regular loops—it rolls right in and goes right back out. The biggest thing is if you accidently reel the knot past the rod tip, like when the guide is trying to grab a tarpon, for instance, it's not going to make any difference—it won't hurt you or your rod. Plus, I'm lazy and I don't really fish for records, so it works for me," Terry says with a laugh.

"It's easier than some of the conventional knots used for a tarpon leader. I've tied it more than a Huffnagle, and it's quicker than a Bimini Twist, so I'm pretty pragmatic and this is quick and easy. It also helps your fly track straighter and helps the leader turn over when you cast. The knot makes a very accurate presentation."

Here's a bonus tip

When you need to tie the braided fishing line to a fluorocarbon or monofilament leader, Terry recommends using back-to-back Uni-Knots. "I do a lot of spin-fishing with light, finesse lures.

That's something we do here in the Indian River Lagoon (in Florida). We use really light braid, like eight-pound, and light or medium-action spinners. If you tie the Uni-Knots right, the knots are pretty slim. I double the braid over with a Spider Hitch, and then I tie a back-to-back Uni with the braid and the leader. The trick is to not use any more than three turns on each side and to make sure they cinch down tight on both ends. They should look like two beer kegs standing on top of each other, perfectly, once you're done tying them. This doubles the abrasion resistance of your braided line, too. I've pulled some snook from places I never thought I'd get them out of, using this knot setup."

Snell

1. Thread the tag end of your tippet up through the hook eye, run it through about a foot, and then circle it back through, so you form a circle around the hook, as shown here.
2. Rotate the loop around the hook shank six times, working back toward the bend of the hook. Use your fingers to pinch the wraps on the hook shank. Really, you're twisting the loop around the hook shank, six times. Slip the wraps up to the hook eye, making sure they stay in orderly wraps.

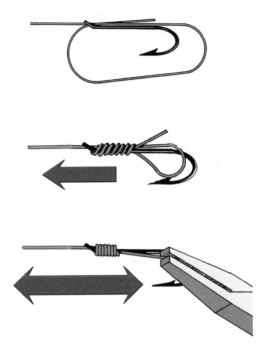

3. Make sure the standing line exits through the hook eye, so the hook tracks straight when you retrieve it. Hold the tag end and pull the standing line to seat the knot. You want an orderly bunch to wrap right behind the hook eye. Clip the tag end.

Non-slip Shoelace Knot

Here's another fun knot to learn. You can use it to tie shoelaces so the laces won't slip on you, or you can secure items with eyelets (like buoy floats maybe?) with this knot. It's good for general joinery.

1. Cross one line over the other—think like you are tying your shoes.
2. Now double the tag end to make a loop and bring the other tag end around in front of the loop.

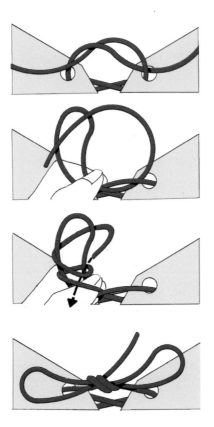

3. Wrap the tag end around the loop. After you've made a couple wraps, bring the tag end down through the wraps you just made.

4. The finished knot will have two bows—the "bunny ears" your mother told you about when she was teaching you to tie your shoes!

Tandem Hook Rig

1. Pass the leader through the hook eye of the first hook. You want to leave a lot of line behind the hook, to work with.
2. Make an overhand knot in the line behind the hook, and draw it into a figure eight around the hook. Bring the loops of the figure eight over the hook point and slowly tighten the knot behind the hook eye.
3. Measure an adequate distance for the fishing you have planned, and tie on a second

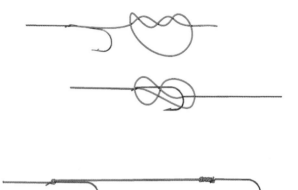

hook, using the terminal connection of your choice, such as the ever-reliable Improved Clinch Knot that we covered earlier in this book.

Berkley Braid Knot

On page 120 in this book, we call this knot the Braided Knot. But it's also identified as the Berkley Braid Knot. So we mention it again, this time recommended solely for use for super-braid lines. This knot was a winner in the popular video series *Knot Wars* hosted by Steve Pennaz. It's particularly effective when used as the terminal connection joining super braid to a hook.

Eugene Bend Knot

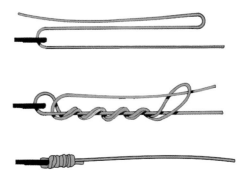

This knot comes to us by way of a recommendation from a fishing-line manufacturer, namely Berkley. They make the lines, test the strength of the lines, and they constantly test knots tied with the lines. The Eugene Bend Knot works in monofilament and fluorocarbon when you have more stiffness to work with, making the loop wraps easier.

1. Pass the tag end of the tippet or leader through the hook eye and make a long loop above the line, as shown here.
2. Wrap the loop around the standing line four times.
3. Bring the tag end through the loop at the end of your wraps.
4. Moisten and carefully draw the knot tight. Clip the tag end.

Bloody Simple Knot

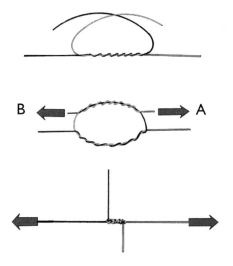

1. The leader pieces overlap and are twisted together.
2. Wrap Tag A over standing line B and loop Tag A around. Tag B wraps around standing line A.
3. Hold the tag ends and the standing line, moisten the wraps, and pull to tighten the knot.

Contributor Biographies

J. M. Chico Fernandez

Chico Fernandez was born in Cuba and moved to South Florida at a young age. With him he brought his love for fishing and began fly fishing in Miami after meeting Flip Pallot. Chico began his career as an accountant and budget director for Burger King, but after a short time he left the corporate world to become involved in the outdoors and fishing fields. This included writing, teaching, and consulting on all things saltwater fly fishing. He has broken and held several world records, including the largest redfish taken with a fly rod, and was the first angler to land a white marlin on a fly. Chico is a steward of conservation and is a strong supporter of Bonefish & Tarpon Trust. He lives in Miami and teaches the joys of saltwater fly fishing to others.

Jerry Gibbs

Though he's chased virtually everything with fins for thirty-five years as *Outdoor Life*'s fishing editor, these days Jerry Gibbs's focus is on striped bass in Maine's Casco Bay during the season, while scheming ways to travel south when the fish do. Of the dozens of mistakes that can be chalked up to angler error, Gibbs admits a personal pet peeve is a poorly tied knot. "There's really no excuse for coming up with a curlicue line end where there once was a hook—and a fish. That translates to poor workmanship. Doesn't matter who you are, one thing you just can't buy is a good knot." Following twenty-four years living, fishing, and hunting in Vermont's Northeast

Kingdom, Gibbs now resides on the Maine coast with his wife Judy and his French Brittany, Jack.

Jimmy Houston

Known as "America's Favorite Fisherman," Jimmy Houston has appeared on television fishing shows for decades. A crowd favorite at bass tournaments and at personal appearances, Jimmy represents many of America's top outdoors-related companies. He is well known as the hardest-working fishing pro in the country. Since winning the Oklahoma State Championship as a college senior in 1966, Jimmy has gone on to win more than a million dollars in bass tournaments. He has fished more than a dozen BASSMaster Classics and won the B.A.S.S. Angler of the Year title in both 1976 and 1986. He has been inducted in many angling halls of fame, and still fishes the FLW Series.

Phil Monahan

A former fishing guide in Alaska and Montana, Phil was an editor at *Outdoor Life* and the editor of *American Angler* magazine. Now the editor of the Orvis Fly Fishing blog, he enjoys fishing the small streams near his home in southern Vermont and traveling across the country reporting on fly-fishing developments.

Sandy Moret

Born in Atlanta in 1946, Sandy moved to Miami in 1972 and fell in love with the Florida Keys and Everglades. He has been Grand Champion of the Keys' most prestigious fly tournaments eight times and is often seen as a guest angler on *Walker's Cay Chronicles*, *The Reel Guys*, and *Andy Mill's Sportsman's Adventures*. Sandy is author of many articles on saltwater fly fishing and has fished and explored extensively throughout the Bahamas, Central America, the Seychelles, Christmas Island, and Palau. He also helped pioneer Russian Atlantic salmon fishing on the Kola Peninsula. Sandy has served on many elected and appointed positions for Everglades's restoration and is a founder and advisory board member of Bonefish and Tarpon Trust, and past chairman of the Don Hawley Foundation. He and his wife Sue live in Islamorada, where they operate Florida Keys Fly Fishing School and Florida Keys Outfitters.

Flip Pallot

Flip was born and raised in South Florida. An avid outdoorsman, Flip began his career as a banker for "way to long," he says. After finding the courage to leave the corporate world, Flip began his second career as a fishing and hunting guide. After twelve years, Flip moved to television producing and sharing his life's fishing travels for us to enjoy. He is best known for *Walker's Cay Chronicles*, which aired for sixteen seasons on ESPN, and he's a founder of Hell's Bay Boatworks. His keen sense for storytelling and bringing to life the best part of fishing adventures has continued with teaching instructional classes and writing books on fly fishing. Flip currently lives in Mims, Florida, and films shows for *Ford's Fishing Frontiers* on the Outdoor Channel.

Peter Corbin

Peter Corbin is primarily known for painting fly-fishing and upland hunting scenes—subjects that mirror his passions. He gives life to sporting land-scapes, merging natural wonders and the drama of memorable moments in sporting life, rendered in pleasing color palettes. His vivid sporting-art scenes convey a sense of place, mood, and atmosphere in the light reflected off the water or the transmitted light through the clouds or trees, revealing influences of the Hudson River School. His greatest influences are A. B. Frost, Ogden Pleissner, and Winslow Homer. He grew up in a home filled with fly rods, shotguns, Labrador retrievers, and sporting art. Inspired by his experiences as a lifelong angler and hunter, he has traveled from the American West, British Columbia, South America, Europe, New Zealand, Africa, and the tropics recording portrait commissions for his clients' love of the outdoors and the places they cherish. He lives in upstate New York.

Terry Gibson

Terry Gibson, of Jensen Beach, Florida, has fished in southeastern waters since the late 1970s, and has dived in and surfed on them for almost as long.

As a journalist, Gibson has reported on fishery and coastal-management issues in most coastal US states and more than twenty countries. Terry also served in editorial positions at *Saltwater Fly Fishing* magazine, *Florida Sportsman*, and as fishing editor for *Outdoor Life*. In 2006, the Florida Wildlife Federation awarded him the Burk "Biff" Lampton Conservation Writer of the Year award. He serves as a fishing consultant to national conservation groups.

Tom Keer

Award-winning outdoor writer Tom Keer has published thousands of freelance works in print magazines, newspapers, digital publications, and blogs. He has won more than thirty awards for his features, columns, and blogs from the Outdoor Writers Association of America (OWAA), the Professional Outdoor Media Association (POMA), and the New England Outdoor Writers of America (NEOWA). He is a member of the board for both OWAA and NEOWA. More recently, Tom has edited magazines such as USA Today *Hunt and Fish*.

He is the author of *The Fly Fisher's Guide to the New England Coast*. He lives with his family and English setters on Cape Cod, Massachusetts.

Steve Pennaz

A resident of Independence, Minnesota, Steve has spent thirty years in the sportfishing industry where he has inspired, educated, and entertained millions of people through print, social media, and the airwaves. Steve got his start in 1988 as the executive director of the North American Fishing Club. He served more than fifteen years as an editor for the *North American Fisherman* magazine, served as a board member of conservation groups such as Wildlife Forever, and is a freelance writer contributing to some of the most prestigious outdoor-industry magazines, including *In-Fisherman, Bassmaster*, and *Outdoor Life,* as well an award-winning television host. In March 2017, Steve was inducted into The Fresh Water Fishing Hall of Fame, the headquarters for education, recognition, and promotion of freshwater sportfishing based in Hayward, Wisconsin.

Author Biography

Joseph B. Healy served as editorial director of *Saltwater Fly Fishing* and *American Angler*, and was editor-in-chief of *Fly Tyer*. He also was associate publisher of *Fly Rod & Reel* and vice president/ editor-in-chief of *Vermont Magazine*. He lives with his family in Northern Vermont.